Racing
Toward
God

The Life Story of
Jerry D. Kaifetz, Ph.D.

To Mrs. Marisa,

Jerry Kaifetz

John 6:68

Jn. 6:68

INTRODUCTION

This is my life story. You may find that it reads like fiction, perhaps improbable, and maybe somewhat embellished. In fact, it is none of these. This is a true account of my life, and details the transformation that took place in a young ski racer who lived an exciting life on a world-wide stage seeking only good times, speed, and adrenaline.

How does a young kid living in Paris, born into a Jewish family of intellectuals and educators find himself in the doorway of a Southern California home speaking to a couple of Christian ladies who took of their time to bring a perfect stranger a message of redemption and hope that would change his life forever?

How does a 21 year old, pot smoking, cocaine snorting, LSD popping Hippy in San Francisco in the 1960's go from a determined and serious study of Eastern Mysticism to an understanding of God's message of salvation and grace through Jesus Christ?

How does a professional American skier in the Swiss Alps give up the Five Star Hotels, summers on the French Riviera, a bungalow on an island jewel in the Caribbean to bring the message of Jesus Christ to the ghettos of Chicago?

That improbable path is my story. It has been heard in thirty-seven countries by three million people and translated into twelve languages, and broadcast on 2,600 radio stations. I hope that in it you will find inspiration and hope. Most of all, I hope that you will make your own the understanding that each and every one of us is loved by our God who first and foremost has chosen to be identified by the world as a loving Father. This is the story of how that great love was personalized for me, and how my life has been transformed beyond description by that experience.

1

The French Connection

I was born in Paris, France. My mother was French and the first war bride to come to the United States after WW II. My father was an American G.I. during WW II and his unit was the recipient of two Bronze Stars. I was born just a few years after the war.

My dad - Lou Kaifetz

My mom - Janine

Paris has long been the culture capitol of the world. It is there that the West's fashion is shaped by a disproportionately influential and small group of misfit homosexuals. Their influence on the world is a phenomenon I will never understand. It all has to do with people being successfully talked into throwing away perfectly good clothes long before they wear out. Their leverage over us is our insecurity over the acceptance granted to us by others and is always based on the most superficial of elements. Having lived in their city, I have never understood granting them the influence in my life that so many easily do.

I learned French before I learned English. I spoke both languages by age six. I spent my youth being educated in French and American public schools.

My Mémé and me in Paris

The French schools were a good four to five years ahead of American schools, and that was in the fifties and sixties when our schools were quite decent. Catching up with the French schools was an extraordinary challenge for me as a boy. After the first grading period in the 4th grade, I was

42nd in a class of 45, and I was working my hardest. My grandmother tutored me daily and by the end of the school year I was third in my class and won an academic award. Much of what I learned in the 4th grade there I didn't get until high school in the U.S..

1st grade in Paris

I always loved my years in the U.S. way more than the years I spent in Europe, although I am grateful for both. My maternal grandparents were educators and intellectuals. I spent a lot of my days off from school with my grandmother in the museums and historical sites of Paris.

Jerry on the Eifel Tower

She was a walking encyclopedia of European history and could wax eloquent on any person, period or place for twenty minutes at the drop of a hat. The lessons I learned from her have colored much of my world view. I see events within a much broader context than I would have been able to otherwise. That is true to this day.

My grandma - Hélene Bonnet

We spent one summer in France in a 400-year old farmhouse, named Chazeyrolette, owned by one of my grandmother's friends from teacher's college in the 1920's. My grandmother was born in 1900. The farm had no modern implements. The hay was cut with long sickles and loaded onto ox-drawn carts by hand. The farmhands made their own rakes from wood. The closest village was about an hour's walk. It was in the mountains and they stayed snowed in all winter. It was the kind of summer from which childhood dreams are woven. We spent another summer in an Atlantic resort on France's West coast, and others at a family villa on the French Riviera providing even more material from which to weave those childhood dreams. The villa was just outside of Grasse, the perfume capitol of the world. As kids, we would harvest Lavender from the foothills of the Alps on which the property was located and bring them to the perfume factory to sell for spending money.

The French Riviera

2

America and Beyond

My other life in the U.S. was a typical small town boyhood dream. We lived on Lake Champlain in close proximity to the mountains, not far from Lake Placid. The sport of Alpine skiing soon took center stage in my life. I was always blessed with athletic talent. I loved football, baseball and basketball, but I did best in wrestling and track in high school. Surely skiing was by far my favorite sport, even though I won a state championship in track at age 16 and set an unofficial world record in another sport that same year. I skied almost every day, as a small ski area nearby called Beartown was open nights. Saturdays and Sundays were big skiing days. I began competing in junior high school, traveling every weekend to race. A lot of my friends had big time skiing talent. One later won a world championship, so it was a constant challenge for me to be competitive. Nevertheless, I worked my way up to a respectable international F.I.S. point level by the time I was in college. After fifteen years of amateur racing I began making a living as professional skier both in the United States and Europe. Skiing was now providing me with an enviable and exciting life. I raced all over Europe in the winter and spent my summers in places like the Caribbean, the French Riviera, and the Red Sea.

My life had always been characterized by what other people would always see as singular and exceptional privilege. I once lived on a Caribbean island. Outside my bungalow was a million and half dollar sailboat – a 128 ft. three-masted racing schooner that had won transatlantic races. Next to it was a 56 ft. Chriscraft with a full complement of diving gear and a diving M.D. and French chef. Next to that were three fast ski boats. All around us were international jetsetters, professional athletes, European models and actresses from many countries. On my boss's birthday we reserved an entire seafood restaurant on the water. The tab came to $30,000. We thought nothing of it. We had grossed six million dollars in five months for the company. Money had absolutely no meaning to me or my friends. People would look at us and ask us in sheer amazement how we ever managed to have the good fortune to live the lives we did. Deep down inside, however, I knew that it wasn't quite what it looked like from the outside. I knew that this wild life couldn't last forever, but I also knew that a part of me didn't really want it to. I just wasn't in very close touch with that part of me yet.

SCUBA diving provided me with great adventures that summer in the French West Indies. I was a certified Master Diver and took full advantage of the indescribable richness of sea life and scenery on the coral reefs that surrounded the island. I went diving almost every day. One of my favorite things was to ask one of the resort's guests to look down at the water when we anchored over a dive site and to guess the depth. They would always say that it looked like about fifteen feet, but that they knew it must be deeper, so they would normally guess about 35 feet. The water was 143 feet deep. You could see the bottom like you were looking into a glass of clear water. In the Red Sea, the visibility was even well beyond that.

My home in Martinique

Chapter

3

Life in the Caribbean

I had a good friend on the Caribbean island of Martinique named Arieh Lobel. Arieh was one of the toughest guys I had ever met. He was Israeli and had been a commando in the Israeli Army. He had a disarming smile that never ceased, had a model's looks and was tremendously popular with everyone, especially the ladies. He was a diving instructor whose deepest dive was more than 330 feet. I wanted nothing more than to make one of those deep dives, so one day Arieh and I struck up a deal: I would teach him to barefoot waterski and he would take me on a 300-foot dive.

Arieh's first barefoot experience did not go well. As he lay stretched out with his hands on the barefoot bar that stuck out the starboard side of the ski boat, we were doing about 40 miles per hour. Next thing you know ... WHOOSH .... there went his shorts! He screamed in his Israeli accent, "JERRY, VAT DO I DO?" I told him to hang on and bring his feet around and start barefooting! We were in a remote lagoon and there wasn't a soul in sight. We were all laughing like crazy when he took my advice. He was "bare"-footing, quite literally! All of a sudden a tremendous spray with the power of a fire hose shot up from his feet and nailed him in the worst imaginable place. He sort of screamed and grunted at the same time as he let go of the bar and bounced along the water like a soccer ball. We turned the boat around and picked him up, still laughing so hard that hauling him back aboard at first seemed like it was going to be a hurculean task. That was the end of Arieh's barefooting days.

About a week later I was on the dive boat with Arieh. There were very few resort guests diving that day, so about three of the Divemasters decided to dive together off Diamond Rock on the Southeast Corner of Martinique where the water was 300 feet deep or more. Arieh invited me to come. We all stepped off the side of the boat and the next thing I knew all of the Divemasters were gone! I saw some bubbles and looked down and there they were, plummeting for the bottom like rocks. I started swimming vertically straight down as fast as I could and I still wasn't catching them. I was equalizing my ears about every second and watching my depth gauge, which was in meters: 40 . . . 45 . . . 50 . . . 55 . . . 60 . . . 65. I had just hit about 200 feet and could now just barely see the divers below me. They were still perfectly vertical and swimming as fast as they could. Then it hit me: this was my deep dive!

We hit the bottom at 270 feet! The accepted limit for sport diving in the U.S. is 100 feet. My mask seemed like it had been pressed onto my face with a vice. I adjusted as best I could to the pressure of about 150 lbs. per square inch on my body. Then we all looked over to our left. Were it not for our regulator mouthpieces, we would have all been gasping in awe of the sight. There was a large fish trap on the bottom about fifteen feet in diameter whose mooring line to the surface had broken. Hoovering over it was the largest Stingray I had ever seen. His wingspan had to be between sixteen and eighteen feet and his stinger looked about three feet long.

His wings hung over both sides of the fifteen foot trap while he tried to get at the fish inside. Instinctively we swam over toward him. We got about halfway there and with one powerful swoop of his giant wings, he was gone. The only problem was that this foray had added exceedingly precious minutes to our bottom time. This was supposed to be a "bounce-dive," as in the days before diving computers, bottom time was always calculated from the beginning of the descent. I had a single tank and everyone else was carrying doubles. I looked at the decompression chart around my neck as we began swimming along the bottom for the boat's anchor to ascend up the anchor line. The trip back up called for a total of 45 minutes of decompression at various depths! I thought for sure I would suck my single tank dry and have to borrow some air before I saw the surface again. Perhaps having been in ski training for six months a year at altitudes of 10,000 feet helped me. Somehow I made it all the way through the decompression stops on my own air. Few divers to this day believe that when I tell them. The experience had been the dive of my life.

One night we were on a night dive about ten miles offshore. I thought for some reason that the darkness of the ocean floor would provide a great opportunity for me to "conquer all fear." We were in about 75 feet of water in a group of about six divers. I let the Divemaster go on ahead with the other divers. I turned my back on them and sat on the ocean floor in a place where I had often seen marine life bigger than I was. Then I turned out my light and gazed into the inky darkness.

I was going to sit there in that blackness until I could completely eliminate all traces of fear from my mind, I thought. The only problem was that my fear grew in intensity rather than diminished. Soon I began to imagine grotesque and monstrous fish faces approaching me with frightening expressions, long fangs and bulging eyes! My heart was beating like a drum! After a while I turned around and could barely discern the lights of the other divers. It is very hard to swim fast underwater, but I probably set a world record rejoining the others.

The whole time, I was absolutely sure that the grotesque monsters were hot on my tail; so real was this perception, in fact, that as soon as I got back in the dive boat I immediately pulled my fins off and looked at them, certain that I would see great bite marks on them from this scary encounter!

A night dive in Martinique

Many years later, a Christian friend and attorney well versed in the methods and tactics of demons would tell me that there was little doubt that this was in fact what these creatures were. Fear is the most powerful of human emotions, which may be why Satan is perhaps most threatened when anyone decides to squarely face their fears.

One day a friend of the family in Plattsburgh, New York who was also a successful attorney (with a Harvard doctorate no less) asked me when I was going to get serious about life. I asked him why I would want to do a thing like that. He said so I could have a successful career and enjoy some stability in my life. I asked him what the most enjoyable time was that he had had in the past year. He said it was a week's vacation at a tropical resort. I answered him that this is the kind of setting where I lived for six months out of every year, and was paid to be there, no less. Why would I want to trade that in to put a suit on every day and only get to be on an island for one week? He didn't have an answer, although a part of me almost wished that he did. It was that part of me with which I was still not in close touch. He looked at me and said, "Jerry, you just need to grow some roots." I still remember my answer: *"I have some roots; I just haven't found a place to put them."*

4

One of the Original Hippies

One patch of soil for those roots that I tried was personally recommended to me by a famous Harvard psychologist of the sixties. His name was Timothy Leary. I was attending a prestigious Eastern Ivy League University and had my encounter there with this high priest of LSD. I took his famous advice to heart: ***"Turn on, Tune in, Drop out."***

That Summer of 1968 I found myself at the corner of Haight & Ashbury in the middle of the 60's Hippie revolution in San Francisco. This was not only a new world for me, but for the entire world as well. We had closely examined the traditional values of our families, our small towns, our teachers and boldly questioned them. To the beat of Beatles music, and others like Jimmy Hendrix and Janis Joplin, we then summarily dismissed those values and unceremoniously booted them off the stage of our lives. Then began the protracted celebration of what we perceived as the greatest cultural victory and awakening of our lives. Fueled with mind-altering drugs and set to the rock beat of many local San Francisco bands who would later be known worldwide, my personal celebration of social and moral autonomy and liberation began.

Seriously seeking for some meaning in life, I sought it in that West Coast rock music scene. I had questioned the societal status quo of the previous generation, then rejected it, then rebelled fully against it. I was arrested in various protests and heard the sobering clang of jail doors slamming behind me for the first time in my life. I thought I had finally found something to believe in. With each acid trip, with each high, I though that the spiritual reality I sought was growing closer. Before long, I saw that this too was an illusion. I had only traded one elusive dream for another. That world into which I had plunged was also an illusion.

Then a hippie friend of mine named Bill Suthard knocked on my door one day. I had known him previously as "Flash," from 545 Ashbury Street. He was all cleaned up now, had short hair and was wearing normal clothes. Most noticeable of all was his big smile and the great energy that he seemed to be beaming out all over. He told me that he had joined a religious order and was studying Eastern religion and had found true peace and happiness there. I could not help but to be taken by the change in him and started coming to some of the classes. Soon I gave away all my worldly possessions and joined their group. I studied, read, meditated and worked in their city missions for three years. It was the first time I had ever heard the name of Jesus Christ, other than as a profane expression. "He was one of the great avatars," they told me. I studied the Bahagavatgita, Rosicrucian works, the Kabalah (Jewish mysticism), and even wrote my own paraphrased version of the New Testament to help me understand it better. After three years, I could see that the answers I sought were not to be found within this group either, and despite a measure of gained enlightenment, I left.

I bought a truck and started traveling all over the country delivering campers. I spent many nights in beautiful settings around the entire United States. I seemed no closer to the truth than ever before. I then took some time off and went back to Europe. I found myself in our family's lovely

Mediterranean villa on the French Riviera, and I hoped that this would be a good place gather my thoughts.

Our family villa in Grasse

Chapter

5

Overlooking the Mediterranean

One day I got in the car and drove by myself to Nice. From Nice I started to drive up into the mountains. This region is called the "Alpes Maritime" because the mountains come right to the sea with no coastal plain. On the highest of the three roads above Nice called the Corniche, I parked the little red Maserati-Citroen and walked to the edge of the road. I was 4,500 ft. above the Mediterranean and I could see more than a hundred miles out to sea from the "Grande Corniche."

It was sunset, and the spectacle was breathtaking. I had never seen as many vivid colors in any sunset as the sun slowly dipped from the western sky into the waiting, multicolored sea. I was awestruck by that brilliant spectacle. Inside me, however, was an empty and haunting feeling. I felt closer to God at that moment than I ever had before. I knew that only an all-powerful, magnificent and universal God could have created such a gorgeous world as I then gazed upon from that lofty perch. I was deeply disturbed as well, however, for ***I knew that I did not know the God who had painted this wondrous tableau before my eyes***. Not only did I not know Him, but I felt the presence of an impenetrable wall separating me from Him. I knew that as long as I lived on my side of that wall, my life would lack the meaning I sought to give it. I had no earthly idea how to get through that wall. I did not know one person to ask. I did not know one book to read. I did not know one place to go to find out. I did not know one person on the other side of that wall, but, oh, how I wished that I did! This was the most beautiful scene I had ever seen, yet I was deeply troubled by my thoughts. It was perhaps the saddest day of my life.

My life from then was no more spiritual than before. It was not as if I knew the path to knowing God or how to get closer to Him and was making any progress along that path. I did not know the way. I was disconnected from God, and there grew in me a sense of increasing resignation. I knew that the next move had to be God's. I came to be fairly well adjusted to this concept, as I have never been much of a hand-wringer. I felt that I was without any other option. If God wanted a relationship with me or wanted me to be closer to Him, He would have to show me the way.

Chapter

6

The Swiss Alps

I came back from a winter of skiing in Europe in the early eighties. I had just spent six months living out the greatest fantasy of my lifetime. The greatest of all my dreams growing up and skiing the Adirondacks as a boy had been to ski the mountains of Switzerland. Places like Davos, Zermat and St.Moritz had been legendary and almost mystical to me. That winter in Europe, I lived in a luxury hotel actually located on the side of a Swiss mountain in Southeastern Switzerland. I had a season pass good at 27 ski areas including Davos and St. Moritz. I worked for the most prestigious ski school in the world, the E.S.F., or French Ski School. I was the only American in that region, and although I missed speaking English, for a dedicated, life-long skier this was nothing short of living in paradise.

The tree line extended only to about 6,000 feet and the mountains were more than 11,000 feet high. That meant that powder skiing in "bottomless powder" was in daily abundance above the trees in unending Alpine meadows below the brilliant, blue Alpine skies with the sun ablaze almost every day.

Those were superb skiing experiences in which one comes as close to being free of the effects of gravity as seemed possible as we drifted down mountain after mountain, sometimes even taking a native guide to reach the more remote places of the Alpine back country. In one valley we came across the peak of a roof sticking out of the snow. The guide told us that it was the peak of a two-story shepherd's summer house. The snow there was almost thirty feet deep!

Ski instructor days in Switzerland

On top of all this I was able each week to test my racing skills against some world-class ski racers, a number of whom were right off the World Cup Circuit. After 25 years on skis, 15 of them in competition, I was challenged and tested as never before. I even spent a few weeks training with several World Cup teams on a downhill course on a French glacier that gave a new definition to what I had previously thought of as "fast." The friction from the ice was actually melting grooves in the bottom of our skis as speeds in excess of 85 m.p.h. were a daily occurrence. I also had the privilege of training with one of the greatest ski racers of all time, Henri Duvillard, who was coaching the Dynastar Pro Team on the Tignes glacier and staying in our hotel.

I somehow soon knew my skiing career was winding down, but when I came back to the United States, I thought I would give it one more year. I had job offers at more than thirty well-known ski resorts stateside. I was in great demand with my credentials from the French Ski School. I settled on the Sierra Nevada range in Northern California. I enjoyed my winter there, especially the trips around to the northern side of Lake Tahoe to ski Squaw Valley and Alpine Meadows. This was as close as I had come in the U.S. to the delights of the Swiss Alps. There were some avalanche chutes in the Sierras that were so steep that they couldn't even hold snow until the Spring. You could peer over the edge and look between your ski tips on these 75 degree pitches and see all the way to the bottom.

A pro ski race in Livigno, Italy

I couldn't get enough of this kind of skiing. There was nothing I enjoyed more than being challenged, or skiing something that others said could not be skied. The term "extreme skiing" was yet to be invented, but it was in my blood, and I guess it still is. I was happiest when the adrenaline flowed like a river in my body. I can personally attest to the fact that the human body has a threshold of adrenaline flow beyond which consciousness cannot be maintained. If you ever get there, look down; you will see my footprints.

Even all these years later, I can't say that this addiction has diminished much; I have just learned to be content keeping it on a shelf longer. Put me on a pair of skis on a big mountain, and that adrenaline pump still works just fine, thank you. With the great advances in the skiing equipment of today, I honestly feel that decades later, I haven't lost much at all when it comes to skiing.

A ski race in Michigan in 2010

Chapter

7

Southern California

After that season in the Sierras, I moved to Southern California. I had finally decided to give up skiing and ski racing, the sport that had provided me with a lifestyle that most people have only imagined. In all of this, however, there was still a sense of emptiness that was now growing into frustration at having reached thirty years of age and still not having any real answers to the great questions of life: Who am I? Why am I here? Where am I going? How do I get there? Not long before that, I had spent a winter working as a professional ski patrolman and doing mountain rescue. I had become an E.M.T. to get this job and I loved it. I had also done some of this kind of work in Europe, which included the use of explosives in avalanche control. We worked with plastic explosives to trigger avalanches in Valbella, Switzerland. Often I would be in the local taverns until after 2:00 a.m. listening to "oompah music" and consuming native beverages, only to get a radio call and go from there right to the patrol shack to load up with 75 pounds of one kilogram bombs and head up a 10,000 ft. mountain in the dark or often in a mountain blizzard to be able to start blasting at daybreak. I couldn't imagine to save my life how anyone could ever put on a suit and tie and work behind a desk for forty hours each week. That would have been a death sentence to me back then. In fact, my life's motto back then pretty much reflected just that sentiment: **"NEVER TRUST ANYONE OVER 30 OR UNDER 6,000 feet!"** This life seemed all behind me

31

now as I settled in Southern California. After a business venture marketing video equipment to professional sports teams, I went to work in the sales force of a solar energy company in San Diego. I did very well and only worked about a dozen hours a week. I met a fellow there who was also very good at what he did. One month the two of us were responsible for 70% of the company's sales. It didn't take us long to realize that we should start our own company. We did just that and became successful very quickly. Neither of us was very motivated to earn a lot of money. We enjoyed our work greatly. It actually became our principal form of entertainment as well as our livelihood. We both developed roughly the same "business plan." We would work for a few weeks, maybe up to two or three months at the most, stick a pile of money in the bank, then take about six months off. I had a nice boat by then and would be on the waters of San Diego Bay almost daily cruising with my friends and ski jumping. I also had a nice garden in the back yard of my house on a Southern California hillside. I would from time to time go back to Europe for few weeks at a time to visit family in Paris and on the Riviera and get my fill of my favorite foods and to soak up some French culture. I loved to take the train from Cannes across the Italian border to a little town and duty-free port on the Mediterranean called Vigntimillia. There was an open air market there every Thursday featuring Italian goods on a level of quality and value that made for one phenomenal shopping experience. I still miss that place.

Vigntimilla, Italy

Chapter

8

Sitting in My Garden

After a while I began to sit by the garden and to do more and more reading and pondering. For the first time, my reading began to include some theology books. I was particularly taken by Dietrich Bonhoeffer's book, "The Cost of Discipleship." I believed that any spiritual truth to be found would be found outside the mainstream of Christian orthodoxy, and the title of this book intrigued me.

I put an ad in the paper around then to sell several pairs of racing skis. A girl called me and asked me about them. They were U.S. Team skis provided to me by K2 Skis, and not sold to the general public. She began to ask me questions, one thing leading to another, and soon I was telling her about my racing experience in Europe. She nearly gasped as she then excitedly began to tell me about a ski team that she was on that competed every week in the mountains of Southern California. She begged me to please come with them just once and race. I told her I wasn't interested. Soon others from that group began to call me. I agreed to go, but just for "one race." They gave me my bib on race day and soon I was at the top of a hill looking down at a dual slalom. When my number was only a couple away, the old adrenaline started pumping once again. I asked myself how I could really give this up.

Then I was in the starting gate listening to the starter's cadence: ***"Racer Ready! Ten seconds. Five, four, three two one ... !"*** I rocked back on the odd numbers, forward on the even, just like the old days. On "one" the tails of my skis shot straight up behind me as I leaned out over my poles ready to snap my body through the electronic starting gate. I then knew the answer to my question: I was not yet ready to give this up!

I raced for two more years in California. My last race was momentous, but I'll share that a little later. It was Spring now in Southern California. My mind went back to another Spring not many years back. I had found myself then on top of a 12,000 foot mountain early one morning. On one side, I could see almost all of the Grand Canyon and all the way to Nevada. On the other side I could see Utah and a corner of Colorado and New Mexico. Ahead of me lay a high desert for a couple of hundred miles to Southern Arizona. The mountains were covered with spring snow, but the valleys below were a lush green. The air was warm.

Skiing Powder at 12,000 ft.

I was greatly moved by the magnificence of this spectacle. Then it happened once again: that same haunting thought returned that had gripped my mind and heart years ago while watching the sun set into the Mediterranean from the side of another mountain six thousand miles away. Once again ***I knew that I did not know the God who had painted this wondrous landscape before me!*** **Who was He? What did He want with me? What did He want me to do with my life?** I just didn't know. Worse, I had no discernible prospects for finding out. I took my skis off my shoulder and tossed them down on the brilliant white corn snow and snapped my feet into the bindings. I pointed them down one of my favorite avalanche chutes, but the joy and the exhilaration had given way to that old, haunting question: **who is this God, and what does He want with me?** Then I remembered something: this was Easter morning. It was as if God was almost rubbing it in: **"You don't know me, do you hot shot? Yes, you have the world by the tail. You have been everywhere; you have done it all. But what does it mean if you don't know Me, Jerry?"** It meant nothing. <u>My life had a gigantic void right in the middle, and it was in the shape of the God I did not know</u>.

Another year passed, filled with the normal ups and downs of life, but generously salted with the excitement of living in Southern California with all of the toys that a young, "successful" single man cherishes. Among these was a very, very fast motorcycle capable of speeds over 150 m.p.h. and the ability to do zero to sixty in 2.8 seconds. The hills and coastline of Southern California provided some world-class experiences for me as I rode for hundreds of miles every week just seeing the sights and enjoying the sun and fresh air. Business was good, I had lots of friends, a fast boat, an open boat-tailed roadster with a big engine, and a pick-up truck. The boat was a 16-foot jet boat with a 455 hp. V8 engine. On top of all this, my yearly vacation days still outnumbered my actual work days by somewhere around five to one.

Then, as spring came again and the winter rains gave way to weeks on end of cloudless skies and balmy breezes, I began to read even more. Theology was all that interested me now. I knew that somewhere in all those books lay the grains of truth with which I desperately wanted to structure some satisfying insights to the old questions that always seemed to return to challenge mind and heart.

Chapter

9

Back to San Francisco

With Easter of 1983 approaching, I decided to make a pilgrimage of sorts back to San Francisco. This was the only place that I had ever encountered people whom I considered to be sincerely religious. On top of that, they were anything but orthodox in their views, which to me back then was a very good thing. I packed a duffle bag and climbed on my motorcycle and headed up the coast.

Easter services there were what most would consider to be very unusual. There was lots of meditating, lots of New Age jargon in the air, but the one at center stage at Easter was still Jesus Christ. The principal message was on the resurrection and its great significance. I remember sitting down with one of the leaders of this group who had known me a dozen or more years before when I was a part of their group. I told him of my unsettled spiritual condition, and from this most unlikely of sources came the most important advice I had ever received in my entire life. He told me to go back home and to find a "good local church" and join up!

I felt thoroughly let down. To me, the words "good" and "church" simply didn't belong in the same sentence. I was raised in the Jewish faith. The only concept I had of church was of the Catholic variety and I knew I didn't want any part of that. I had been in many of the great cathedrals of Europe and could not envision being a part of any of it. I knew that their God was not the one I sought. My Jewish faith had never connected me to God in a way that satisfied either. This sentiment seemed to prevail with our family's many close Jewish friends. For them, Judaism was much more of a cultural and social expression, evoking the Jewish traditions and history. That was supposed to be my faith, but I never reached God in Judaism the way that I believed was possible. Moreover, I sadly never met anyone who was able to convey to me that they had reached God and truly knew Him.

I thanked my friends in San Francisco for their warmth, concern and hospitality and for a great Easter service. The day after Easter, I got back on my motorcycle and headed south down Highway 1. With the cliffs, giant Pacific surf and the rocks of Big Sur as the background, I still had the sounds of Handel's Messiah echoing in my mind and heart as I made the journey home astride the big bike, leaning in and out of the serpentine turns on the most spectacular coastal highway in the world.

I pulled into my driveway early that evening. Around ten o'clock, I decided to go to bed. Then I remembered the advice about finding a church. I reasoned that there were thousands of churches and that the percentage of good ones was undoubtedly minuscule, if indeed there were any at all. I was not going to go on some kind of long campaign of visiting a bunch of dried up, churches full of nothing but dogma, ritual or hype. Nevertheless, it seemed as if God had hit the ball into my court, albeit not in anything resembling a serious or challenging manner, I thought. So by the side of my bed at about ten o'clock that night, I knelt down and I prayed this prayer: ***"Dear God, if there is a church out there that You want me to go to, let me know which one and I'll go. Amen!"*** I climbed in bed without another thought on the subject and was soon fast asleep.

I was in my early thirties then. I had lived anything but a sheltered life. I had been to the Middle East, all over Europe, the Caribbean, Canada, Mexico.   Not ONCE had anyone ever approached me to tell me anything of Jesus Christ or to inquire as to my spiritual condition. Dividing one into the total days of my life, the odds of anyone doing that in answer to that evening's prayer were in excess of 10,000 to one, I reasoned.

The following day was Tuesday. I got up early, made a cup of coffee and went out by the garden to read. I had come back in the house at ten o'clock, when I heard a knock at the door. It had been exactly twelve hours since I had prayed my prayer to God, thinking that I had hit the ball back into His court, and was now free to live as I always had.

I went to the door, and as I opened it, I saw two ladies standing there smiling at me.   They were both nicely dressed, and each one carried a Bible. One was a little older than the other. She looked right at me, smiling, and made the following short speech: "Hi. I'm Betty and this is Darlene. We are from a small Baptist church down the street and we came by to invite you to come and visit us this Sunday."

Betty Storie, the Lady who put my hand in God's

In my stunned silence, **I could not deny for one second that God had just miraculously answered my prayer!** If He had appeared in a cloud or a whirlwind of fire, that experience could not have been more real or powerful to me. I knew beyond the shadow of a doubt that God had sent those two ladies in a way that was no different from the way He sends angels to do his bidding on earth. I read volumes into their mere presence at my door. It was as if God had just opened a door that had been closed all my life. Not knowing what else to say, I simply said, "I'll be there." They were so surprised they literally did not know what to say.

All during the week I called friends and told them they were coming to church with me on Sunday. I was not going there to "check it out." That little Baptist church had God's seal of approval on it, sight unseen, as far as I was concerned. On Sunday, I walked in and sat down. I could, to this day, take you to the very seat. That day Pastor Dorman Owens preached and in his message, validated everything I had expected to find in that little church. He was a man anointed of God, preaching God's message in the power of God's Spirit. **I knew the moment I heard him speak with an authority I had never before heard, that whatever he had was that for which I had searched the world. I wanted it, and I would do whatever was necessary to have it. God had answered my prayer, and I knew it.**

That week, Pastor Dorman came to my house to pay me a visit. How he was able to wade through my convoluted theology to determine my spiritual condition was a minor miracle in and of itself. Somehow he did though, and explained to me how to be reconciled to a holy God.

I understood for the first time in my life that God's standard was perfection, or He could not be God. I saw that I had not, nor could I ever rise to that standard. **Then he explained to me how God had made a provision to literally cover my sins through the death of Jesus**

Christ on the cross as the only payment He could accept for my sins: His own Son. The light shone in!

With all of my heart and soul, I put my faith in the death of Jesus Christ on Calvary's cross as my substitute to forever be the only payment for my sins acceptable by God. God's mercy and justice met for me that day. I have not been the same person since.

Soon after that I was baptized in a swimming pool in San Diego and made up my mind that my life now belonged to God to do with as He saw fit from that day forward.

One day the pastor asked me if I wanted to go "visiting" with him. I said "sure." I found out that this was something he did every week. He would drive to a middle class neighborhood, park his car and just start knocking on doors telling people about Jesus Christ. Soon I saw some of these folks come to church, just as I had. Soon I saw miracles occur in their lives and in their families. I saw families blessed, I saw broken lives mended, I saw despair replaced by joy and hope. I had been in the Ivy League schools, I had studied all of the social sciences, and I knew that there was nothing in that academic world that could begin to compare with the healing grace and love of Jesus Christ presented through the influence of a good church. I decided that this would be a priority in my life. My life verse became John 6:18, when Jesus asked Peter if he too would leave Him, and Peter answered,

"To whom shall we go? Thou hast the words of eternal life."

EPILOGUE

One day my phone rang. It was a friend telling me of a pro ski race in the mountains. He reminded me that the prize money was good and that there probably would not be anyone racing there that day whom I had not already beaten at least once. I decided to go. This would be my last race, I told myself.

We drove to the mountains on race day. I looked at the course and thought it was tailor made for me: very tight, steep and technical on top and wide open on the bottom. Any mistakes on the top part would be multiplied in speed lost on the bottom. I had skied thousands of race courses just like it.

Before the race, as was my ritual, I skied off into the woods and reached into my parka for a little bottle of Yukon Jack. I always took one big swig just moments before racing to calm my nerves. This time I looked at the bottle, and a voice seemed to be saying, "You don't need that now, Jerry." I stared at the bottle, then threw it in the deep snow. I threw off my jacket, stretched one last time, and skied over to the starting gate. I was in the red course. This was my second and last run. After the first run, I was in second place in a field of over 100 racers. I looked to my right and saw the one racer I did not want to see. He was undefeated in the last three years and the only racer I had not beaten all year. He was also in first place. I did then what I had never done before in the starting gate of a ski race. I prayed: "Dear Lord, help me to ski my best."

When our names were announced as next to go head to head in parallel courses, every eye on the mountain was on the starting gate. Everyone knew this for all the marbles. The starter announced our names and began his routine: "Racers ready! Ten seconds. Five, four, three, two, one, GO!" I had the best start of my life and was barely ahead on the first gate. I risked it all on the top of the course and somehow got a great rhythm going that slung me through the steep, icy gates high and fast and, miraculously, without any mistakes. As the gates snapped by inches from my head, we hit the transition and I thought I was still just barely ahead. Even so, I was not going to risk it by looking. From then on it was just "stay smooth, low and stay over your skis" until the finish line. **The adrenaline was flowing like a fire hose!**

As I came to the finish line at a high rate of speed I leaned back and kicked up the tip of my right ski to break the beam of light. I made a giant turn, snow spewing everywhere as I came to a stop, thighs on fire and gasping for breath. Before I was even stopped and before the times were announced, my friends swarmed me amidst shouts and cheers, as we all fell into a big pile on the snow. Then the announcer gave the times. I had won by three one-hundredths of a second! All I could think of was, "Thank you, Jesus!" I knew He had done this for me. **This was far more than a ski racing victory, and I knew it. It was the beginning of a victorious life.**

That summer an evangelist came to our church. I came to him and asked him what I needed to do with my life to learn to serve God. He told me to go to Bible college. I did not hesitate. I knew this was God's call. I sold all that I had, and what I didn't sell I gave away. In the fall of 1983 I headed to Bible College. I graduated in 1986 with a B.S. in Pastoral Theology. In 1988 I graduated from seminary with a Masters degree in the same field. In 1992 I earned a Ph.D. in Philosophy in Religion from another seminary. In 1986 I was awarded the Sword of the Lord Award for Evangelism, having followed Pastor Dorman Owens' example of nearly four decades of sharing his faith weekly. I have never known another Christian so faithful to the Great Commission. Many people are in heaven today because of Pastor Dorman Owens, and pastors are in pulpits and missionaries serve in the field in many places because of his weekly faithfulness to tell people of Jesus and to bring thousands of people the message he brought into my living room in the Spring of 1983.

In 1989 I wrote a book about my exploits and the end result of my life spent searching for God. The book was called *"World Class Truth – Bible Principles in Sports and Adventure."* It has sold many thousands of copies and received much acclaim and the kinds of reviews for which authors always hope. I have written over a dozen books since then, some of which are now with major publishers

I married the only girl I ever seriously dated in Bible college, a union exemplifying far more grace than justice for me. Her name is Gwen. We have been happily married since 1985 and have two grown and married children, Michael and Elisa, whose lives are richly blessed of God. We moved in 2011 from a beautiful home on a 13 acre wildlife preserve in Northewst Indiana with four ponds, trees, walking paths, wildflowers, a fountain and a waterfall. We now live in Weatherford Texas, where I get to enjoy riding a pretty red Harley, called "Little Red Rooster" on Texas back roads and even the occasional jaunt at the wheel of a race car on a local road track. Gwen and I also like to drive my other fun car, a supercharged, midnight blue German roadster, also known to gobble up stretches of North Texas back roads under sunny western skies.

I own Omega Chemical Corporation. We manufacture industrial cleaning products of my own design in Chicago. We sell all over the United States and in several foreign countries.

Of all of the sentiments expressed in the New Testament, undoubtedly the one to which I am disposed to best relate is the expression of the Apostle Paul in Philippians:

**"YEA DOUBTLESS, AND I COUNT ALL THINGS
BUT LOSS FOR THE
EXCELLENCY OF THE
KNOWLEDGE OF CHRIST
JESUS MY LORD: FOR WHOM**

I HAVE SUFFERED [allowed]
THE LOSS OF ALL THINGS, AND DO COUNT
THEM BUT DUNG,
THAT I MAY WIN CHRIST."

And that's my testimony, and I'm stickin' to it .....!

. . . .

Thank you for allowing me the great privilege of sharing my testimony with you, and for taking the time to read it. I hope that you will share it with it others.

Dr. Jerry D. Kaifetz
Weatherford, TX

http://jerrykbooks.com

Blog
http://jerrykaifetz.com

Unshackled Radio Program:
Program no. A2948, 2007 Archives

e-mail:
jk@jerrykbooks.com

VIDEOS

You Tube - Kaifetz - Eagles Canyon Raceway
Kaifetz - Cozumel

OTHER VIDEOS

YouTube.com - Jerry Kaifetz

Other Books by Jerry Kaifetz

The Little Drop of Water who Learned to Give Himself Away
Abeka Books, Amazon Books

The Bench - A Heavenly Coversation
Amazon Books

World Class Truth - Biblical Principles in Sports and Adventure
Amazon Books

Profaned Pulpit - The Jack Schaap Story
Amazon Books

Clouds Without Rain - Spiritual Ineffective Churches and How to Fix Them
Amazon Books

Heroes of the Valley
Coming Soon

Called Unto Liberty - Biblical Light on the Corporate Church
Coming soon

For an audio-visual version of my testimony, go to Youtube.com and type Kaifetz Unshakled

Made in the USA
Monee, IL
03 October 2021